BYRDOLOGY

Just a Couple of Thoughts I Decided to Jot Down

ByrdOlogy

BYRDOLOGY

Published by: 4th and Pine Media

www.jrichardbyrd.com

First Edition, August 2015

Contact the Author

Connect with J. Richard Byrd at speaking@jrichardbyrd.com visit his Website at www.jricharbyrd.com

DEDICATION

This book is dedicated to my late grandparents Dorothy Crowley, Mary E. Clark and Olin Clark.

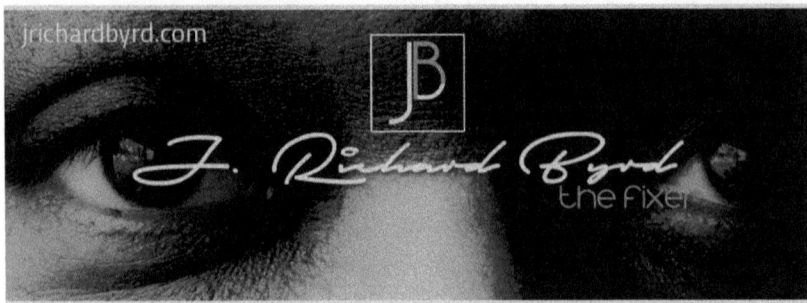

jrichardbyrd.com

J. Richard Byrd
the fixer

ABOUT THE AUTHOR

J. Richard Byrd is a man that loves God, music, and business. He is a highly sought after consultant, speaker, and business coach, specializing in urban marketing, business development, leadership, and church growth.

He has served as a guest lecturer, panelist or workshop facilitator in such prestigious places as, **UCONN, Boston College, Eastern Ct State University, St. Joseph's College, and Wesleyan University.**

His company, the Byrdlogy Group, LLC has designed and consulted some of the largest ministries and companies in the country, such as, **Yolanda Adams, Crystal Aikin, Dr. Jamal Harrison-Bryant, Dr. Rita Twiggs, Rev. Tony Lee, Dr. Frank M. Reid III, Ja'Rule, William Murphy, BlackGospelPromo.com, The Joint College of Pentecostal Bishops, Bishop J. Delano Ellis, the late Bishop Kenneth Moales, Bishop Iona Locke, Dr. Cindy Trimm, Bishop Clifford "Tech-**

norev" Frazier, and Pastor AJ Wright, just to name a few.

It is as a business man that Mr. Byrd has garnered some of his greatest accomplishments. As a principal and COO of the Walker Group of Companies (an entertainment and real estate powerhouse), Mr. Byrd has worked with and advised some of the greatest legends in the entertainment industry, including, **Jamie Foxx, Africa Baambaataa, Dr. Bobby Jones, Donald Lawrence, rapper DMX, Hezekiah Walker, Freddie Jackson, Dr. Shirley Caesar , Twinkie Clark, Forbes Magazine, Foxwoods Casino, and many more.**

Mr. Byrd's past and present clients have garnered over 19 platinum, 40 gold records, and millions of dollars of sales. As an associate producer of the Dr. Bobby Jones Gospel, Live at Foxwoods Series, as seen on the Word Network, Mr. Byrd's television work can been seen in over 54 million households across the US.

Mr. Byrd is an accomplished composer and songwriter whose credits include scoring plays and musicals across the country. Mr. Byrd has performed for heads of state and many luminaries.

CONNECT WITH ME:
Twitter: @ByrdOlogy
Facebook: facebook.com/ByrdOlogy
Instagram: ByrdOlogy
Website: jrichardbyrd.com

Contents

INTRODUCTION

When my grandfather was in the hospital we would visit day in and day out. After each visit to my grandfather I would lean over and tell him *"I Love You"*, his answer would always be the same.

"I appreciate you and Sue taking care of me." In that vein I want to tell all of you – I appreciate you and thank you for taking care of me."

What is ByrdOlogy:

ByrdOlogy is my way of life. It is my way of doing business. It is not science – you won't find it in a schoolbook. It is just some things I have learned from 30+ years of business and life.

Why Write the Book

Over the last 10 years I have gone through major changes and transitions. The deaths of three of my grandparents, Children growing up and leaving the house.

Moving away from everything that made me feel comfortable to a new city where I don't know anyone. Through all of that I have had some wonderful learning experiences that I have written throughout this book.

These are my musing, the stuff I hear in the early morning while praying or meditating.

I have counseled so many people to step out of their comfort zones; To heed the call if you will, To finally do something "unsafe".

To be exposed and To write in incomplete sentences if it makes the point.

What I am saying, sometimes just break the rules; DISRUPT THE STATUS QUO -

I now have to practice what I preach. I am giving you my inner thoughts.

WATERMELON, WATERMELON – (You will get that later.)

Enjoy

WRITE WHAT YOU HEAR

Over the past few days I have had the chance to counsel several people in clearly different and separate fields. In all cases I was led to just say **"Write What You Hear"**.

It is not just a divine directive for those people I spoke to, but a clarion call to myself.

You see for years, I have had ideas and books boiling inside of me. But fear and obstinacy stopped me from heeding the call I heard.

For days, I labor over decision to write something that is rattling around in my brain. But no more. I must now Write What I Hear.

"And Jehovah answered me, and said, Write the vision, and make it plain upon tablets, that he may run that readeth it."
- Habakkuk 2:2

The call I hear is so strong that I have had to stay up late just writing what I hear. Some of it is for public consumption – Other things are a part of the vision God is giving me for my life and for the church he has entrusted me with.

"And it shall come to pass afterward, that I will pour out my Spirit upon all flesh; and your sons

and your daughters shall prophesy, your old men shall dream dreams, your young men shall see visions."   *- Joel 2:28*

Not only must I write what I hear – I have to write what I see. What an awesome responsibility to share with you what I hear and what I see. I have established several writing resources to make writing easier. I will share those with you later -

But more importantly. What has God whispered to you in the middle of the night? In the middle of your quiet time? In the middle of your despair? What is he telling you to Write?

My friend, please just do it – don't hesitate – don't worry about grammar – **Just Write What You Hear. You Down?**

RIP UP THE CARPET

Over the past few weeks I had become despondent over the condition of the carpet in my home. If you know me well, then you know I can get almost OCD when something starts bothering me.

It was affecting my sleep – Affecting how I feel about even coming home. I had to get it fixed before it destroyed my sanity. I went to the carpet store priced out new carpet.

I even rented a steam cleaner. Bought all kinds of cleaners, etc. But something told me to rip up a corner of the carpet. I did that to find gorgeous old hardwood floors.

Who would cover up these floors? Well maybe at the time they needed to be protected. Maybe at the time the occupants needed the warmth. Maybe there was a blemish that someone needed to cover up.

— The moral of the story —

Over the years in your life, you have had to cover up a blemish, or protect yourself, or create warmth with a carpet.

But I am writing to you to say — It might be

time to rip up the carpet and see the beauty that lies beneath.

What you are covering is better than was is covering. As for me: Today I am spending my day ripping up carpet. #ByrdOlogy

THE OLD MAN, THE BOY, AND THE DONKEY

There is an old Aesop Parable told of the Old Man the Boy and the Donkey. It goes something like this.

An old man and a young boy were traveling through their village with their donkey. The boy rode on the donkey and the old man walked.

As they went along they passed some people who remarked it was a shame the old man was walking and the boy was riding.

The man and boy thought maybe the critics were right, so they changed positions.

Later, they passed some people that remarked, "What a shame, he makes that little boy walk." They then decided they both would walk.

Soon they passed some more people who thought they were stupid to walk when they had a decent donkey to ride. So, they both rode the donkey.

Now they passed some people that shamed them by saying, "How awful to put such a load on a poor donkey."

The boy and man said they were probably right, so they decided to carry the donkey.

As they crossed the bridge, they lost their grip on the animal and he fell into the river and drowned.

The moral of the story?

If you try to please everyone, you may as well just kiss your ass goodbye.

MOVING THE BALL

In a college football a young player and another player got into animated discussion on whether it was the receiver or the rushers that were the main catalyst for the team's success.

Each player made their points. The receiver boasted the overwhelming yardage that he had gained through the aerial assault of the team – of all the touchdown passes he had caught.

The rusher countered with all of the yards he had rushed. He boasted of the many touchdowns he rushed, the last minute yardage gained that resulted in a touchdown.

A coach that was sitting nearby heard the discussion, and after listening for several minutes, in disgust walked over and spoke to the two players.

"Son, the point of football is not who scores the touchdowns, but it is how can we as a team move the ball."

I submit to you that as a business movement we have gotten into celebrating the touchdowns but forgotten, the key is just to move the ball. More importantly to move the ball as a team. We only celebrate the big victories, but not the little gains we make to get there.

Take a moment, right now and I mean right now, assess your local movement - are you obsessed with the celebration or are you happy with moving the ball?

LESSON FROM A HOMELESS WOMAN PART 1

My wife and I stopped by the local Starbucks to get a cup of coffee. As we went to our seats, we noticed a young lady sitting at the table next to where we were about to sit. She had her Bible out and she also had numerous bags surrounding her.

As we sat down to have our coffee, we began a conversation with the woman. Her name was Desiree. And, she was homeless. Now, I mention the word homeless, only because it just sets up the story and the situation.

Desiree was a lovely lady who began to share with us her story. As she shared her story, there were some very good life lessons and business lessons that I learned. Honestly, This was one of the best breakfast times I have had in a long time.

So I just wanted to share these lessons I learned from Desiree that day.

1. Never let your situation dictate your outlook.

Desiree was homeless, but her present situation did not cloud the sunny future she saw for herself. She shared with us her dreams and her aspirations. She shared with us her plans on what she was going to be doing in the next 2 to 3 years. Desiree was bubbly and flowing over with enthusiasm about her future.

Take-Home – No matter where you are right now in your business make sure you keep a positive outlook for your future.

2. Break the mold-don't stay in the rut

One of the things, we talked about was how people seem to continue going in circles. How many of the people that she met on a day-to-day basis who were homeless, seemed to think they would always be homeless. Here was Desiree's take on the situations. You have to determine in your mind that you are no longer going to stay where you are. Your future is determined by being able to break the mold.

Take-Home – If you are going to be successful; don't be afraid to get out of your own way. In fact, don't be afraid to break the mold. To bust out of the box. And more importantly, get out of the everyday rut.

3. Suffering is but a moment in the grand scheme of things.

Desiree spoke at great length about where she

was going, about the changes she was making in her life in order to be better. She also spoke at length about the suffering that she was going through in her present situation.

She began to tell us the tale of how she had been homeless for about a year. And that according to her plan she would have to be homeless and another six months to a year to get back on her feet. But what she said after that was mind-boggling.

Desiree said in the grand scheme of her 43 years living, being homeless for two years is just for a moment.

In fact she went Bible on me and said, "If all of my life is suffering, it is still but a moment in eternity."

- Desiree

Take-Home - When we are up against the wall. When we are facing our biggest obstacles. We often huddle down and feel that we are being tried in the fire. If we really think about it, our suffering is just for a small time.

In business, as well as life, we have to go through periods of what we consider to be suffering. The key is to understand that this suffering is just for a moment in the grand scheme of things. We will emerge sooner or later.

There is so much that I learned from Desiree that day. I left much better than I came. I hope to one day run into Desiree after her process so that I can witness the miraculous transition that her journey has brought her.

LESSON FROM A HOMELESS WOMAN PART 2

Backdrop: Yesterday my wife and I stopped by the local Starbucks to get a cup of coffee. As we went to our seats, we noticed young lady sitting at the table next to us. She had her Bible out and she also had numerous bags surrounding her.

As we sat down to have a cup of coffee, we began a conversation with woman. Her name was Desiree. And, she was homeless. Now, I mention the word homeless, only because it just sets up the story and the situation.

Desiree was a lovely lady who began to share with us her story. As she shared her story, there were some very good life and business lessons that I learned. Honestly, This was one of the best breakfast times I have had in a long time. So I just wanted to share these lessons I learned from Desiree that day.

4. Be determined to change the cycle of abuse

Desiree's back story was quite frightening. She spoke to us about being in an abusive relationship, and what she had to endure in that relationship. She spoke on the courage it took for her to walk out of that relationship. I mean the result was hard, She is Homeless. She also spoke of abuse in her family as a child.

What she was determined to do was not allow that cycle of abuse to affect her children. So she courageously walked out the door, even when it was hard.

Take-home- In business your abuse may not be a physical abuse. But you may be being abused by clients that don't pay on time or clients who pay little but demand the most.

You have to have the courage to break the cycle of abuse and walk away. It may not be easy. It may be painful. But you must have courage. Desiree did.

5. Choose to be happy

Now Desiree could've spent all of her time while talking to us, lamenting about her situation. She could have spent her time wallowing in self-pity. But she said to me, I choose to be happy. I choose happiness over sadness.

Desiree recounted a story of how other people she knew in the homeless shelter that would actually get mad at her because she had joy on the inside. She said she told them, you can either be mad and sad at where you are or you can choose to be happy.

Take-home - Everything in your life is not going to be a bed of roses. There are going to be many days in your business when things just don't go right. There are going to be days when you can't seem to make the right decisions.

And if you let that continue to only be your outlook. You're going to end up miserable and hating your business. But what you can do is in your sad times choose to be happy. It will not change the decisions.

They may not even change the situation. But it will change how you process the situation.

6. Choose liberty.

I think this one goes hand-in-hand with choosing happiness. Desiree spoke about leaving her bad situation and moving into a good situation. When posed with the question as to why she would make such sacrifices why would she give up so much **she said I choose to be free.**

Those words resonate in my spirit. I choose liberty.

Take-Home – This one is especially for those

people who are thinking about becoming an entrepreneur, who are thinking about taking the leap into owning a business. The decision may be hard, the obstacles may be high, but I promise the reward is so sweet. Choose liberty.-

I so look forward to that day when I can meet Desiree again, after she's finished her process and see the transition of the transformation this journey has had on her.

Desiree will have a special place in my prayers, I wish she knew how much she changed my life in those 17 minutes we sat talking in a coffee shop.

TRIMMING THE FAT

When I was young, my grandfather took me to a slaughterhouse. Besides being permanently scarred, I found something particularly interesting. If you have never been to a meat market, Go.

One of the amazing things is you can have the butcher cut your meat for you. Most butcher sections of the super market will do this for you. Ok not so amazing, but it was fascinating to me at a young age.

When the butcher cuts your meat, he spend a great amount of time, trimming the fat. In fact, that is what I want to talk about. Trimming the fat.

In every business, ministry or personal lifestyle there is fat. Fat is that stuff we accumulate from time to time until we are so obese we can't function.

Fat can be that extra step put in to the telephone etiquette manual.

Fat can be that set of duplicate files we find on our computers.

Fat can even be that outdated way of doing things that is just not relevant to the way we operate today.

Fat is anything that weighs down your operation and keeps it from being the most efficient or effective it can be.

Every year around this time, I start the process of trimming the fat in my business. Not only in operations, but also in finances. I spend the last few months of the year, redirecting, and repositioning my business for the upcoming year. You can't be successful with bloat, and a lot of extra baggage that you don't need.

This year I thought it would be helpful to you, if I share the process I use to trim the fat, rebrand, and reposition my business, my ministry and my personal lifestyle.

Possibly there will be some tips you can use in your organization. As with anything there may things you can use and some things you can't.

In that case, just eat the meat – and trim the fat.

AM I GOOD ENOUGH

Can I be transparent for a moment? Even with a perceived look of success, I struggle daily with 'am I good enough'?

Am I a good enough business man?
Am I a good enough father?
Am I a good enough communicator?

It is a daily struggle – but somehow I persevere.

How?

I have always been a person who likes facts. I want to judge your fruit, not your talk. So I have the same talk with myself.

Has God blessed you?
Has God shown you favor in places that would have been impossible for you to succeed without Him? Have you seen positive fruits of your labors?

When I answer yes to these questions. I realize that I still have worth, I still have a future and more importantly I am good enough. How do you handle the inner critic?

ARE YOU CARRYING DEAD WEIGHT

Today I continued cleaning out my old server. As a hosting company, I had several hundreds of accounts that I maintained for clients.

Well a few years ago, I moved 90 percent of my accounts to a faster and better server. I only kept a few active accounts on that old server. As I went through the server this morning, I realized that I never deleted the old accounts from the old server. Here was the kicker, I am still paying the leasing fees for that server with all of those accounts. Some are still clients, but most have been terminated or moved.

Can you believe that!!! For years I have been carrying dead weight. For years I have been paying for the dead weight.

What was I afraid of?

I was afraid of losing some things. I was afraid to admit that these accounts were terminated or moved. Secretly I was hoping they would come back. I was betting what if?

Here is what I learned.

When moving up in the world, you can't be afraid to delete some things. You can't be afraid to let some things go. You can't carry people that don't want to support you.

If you want to keep it. Archive it, pack it, and put it away. No reason you have to keep it in your paying platform.

Translation.

While my situation deals with a physical server, you may be having this same issue in your company, your ministry or your life. Your paying platform might be your attention, your employees, or systems that are not working. Are you paying double?

Understand that some dead weight has to be archived, packed, and put away. Ask yourself, **Are you Carrying Dead Weight?**

ORGANIZATIONAL VALUES

Today I am spending some time creating organizational values. Essentially, what is it that my organization values?

So many times in an organization there is what we call an undercover culture. A culture that has developed but does not really align itself with the values of the organization.

This usually happens because the leader has not taken time to really define the values of the organization. Although it seems daunting the process is simple. Here is how I do it.

1. Grab a White Board.

2. Sit with my team – I ask these questions. What is most important to you for this company? What are your "not going theres" ? What do you admire most about the work we do?

What do you want our clientele to take away from this organization? What do you want employees to take away from this organization?

3. Write everything down – It is important that you record all the ideas.

After following this process, I will let the suggestions sit on the board for a few days. This allows it to really get deep in the psyche. I then sit with the suggestions and craft a values statement.

Once we agree, it becomes the Organizational Values. Now this process works for me and the companies/ministries I have consulted.

Do you have Organizational Values?

How do you set-up your Organizational Values?

AUDIT

Today I began the fight to automate, consolidate, and trim the fat from my business, by auditing my business workflows. Now to some, the word audit may be a bad word.

But in this context I assure you it is all good. I started the process today by writing down my daily schedule. This is my audit stage.

You cannot cut if you don't know what are cutting. First I start with my morning ritual and procedures. I take a close look at each process and basically write down each step to a project.

Here is an example.

Morning Twitter Ritual:
   a. Check Direct Messages
   b. Check and respond to all mentions
   c. ReTweet and Schedule 4 or 5 posts
   d. Connect with 5 people new people.

I continue with the process until I have listed all of my morning routine. This process gave me two good things.

   1. Where I am inefficient or efficient.
   2. Where I can make improvements.

Now that I written my procedures – I can decide whether or not to have someone else complete these tasks on a daily basis.

Go ahead and give it a try – you don't have to do it the same as I, but take a minute and audit your workflow.

Message me and let me know how it worked for you or if you think there might be a better way.

MESS UP

Well it has been just under 10 days that we've moved into the new office space. And since this was a major move for me, I prayed, *"Lord just don't let me mess up."* I prayed this prayer everyday.

It is not because I think that I am going to do something so egregious that I am going to bankrupt the business. I just want everything to be perfect.

What I soon realized is that this thinking is what held me back for so long. I was easily falling back into the same habits that have kept me from achieving my greatest levels because I was not messing up, I was being mediocre.

Let me go further. To not mess up means to just do enough to stay where you are. Whenever I've been in any kind of renovation, any kind of remodeling, it meant that I had to make a mess in order to make it better.

I've never taken over any company where I did not have to dismantle something in order to build it better. There's never been a construction site that has not been messy.

Don't get me wrong, I'm not saying don't be organized. I'm saying that sometimes you have to create a mess in order for things to be better.

So my new prayer has been, Lord help me to mess up. Help me to mess up the status quo, help me to mess up standard thinking, help me to mess up just being ordinary.

My friends, I wonder if there's something in your life or in your business you just need to mess up.

CREATE

My hard drive crashed. And while there is a multiplicity of files that I have lost.

What I have not lost is my ability to create. In fact, I can re-create everything that I've lost.

So my friend, as long as you are alive and able to create, don't worry about what you've lost.

IAMGRATEFUL

My time-capsule hard drive crashed and I lost 5 years and 2 terrabytes of design work - but **Byrd-Boy1** texted to tell me that he loves me —

My bills are getting overwhelming – but **Byrd-Boy2** – stops by every night to talk to me about his day —

I felt depleted and that I had nothing else to offer to the world creatively or musically – – but **ByrdBoy3** – called me last night and spent 2 hours talking to me about music and his dreams –

I am still depressed by the death of my grandmother – but **ByrdBoy4** – called to tell me he is in school and we discussed his future —

I spilled coffee in my MacBook Pro — But **ByrdBoy5** – spends the majority of his night making me laugh—

Boyz I Love y'all – you don't know how much you encourage and inspire me daily — **Nyghel Byrd – Jhymel Byrd – Myel Byrd – Patrick Thomas-Byrd – Taviel Byrd**

UPDATE YOURSELF

Many times I turn on my computer to find a warning or alert that it is time for an update. There are many types of updates. Some are security patches. Others are enhancements.

While there are some that are bug fixes. Each update is important because if you don't update, it can leave you in a deficit position.

As I updated my computer this morning, I began to think about my life. Do I need a bug fix, a security patch, or an enhancement. It was a resounding YES.

I wondered why then was I afraid of the changes that would need to happen in order for their to be an upgrade. Why run from the change. Why run from the downtime that it takes to make me a better me.

You know what my friend. There is no reason. In this season of my life, I am learning to embrace the upgrade.

THERE IS A SHAKING GOING ON

I was sipping my coffee the other day remembering a year prior I was making my daily 2-hour train commute.

Although, relaxing in the morning, the trip home in the afternoon, especially on Fridays, would sometimes turn into a 4-6 hour commute.

The platform would be littered with people trying to make it home for the week-end. I would pile myself into the already overstuffed train car; not finding any seats, I would maneuver through people trying to find a little space to breathe.

I would be jostled, pushed, and sometimes stepped on, as the train would lurch from side to side. I would hold on for dear life just to keep from being thrown to the floor.

My only consolation, was knowing that soon I would be home.

Yet again, I find myself being jostled, pushed, and stepped on, by the train of life. I still find that my sole consolation, is knowing that soon I will reach my destination. Friends, there is a shaking going on.

My question to you – Are you willing to Stand

and Hold on until you get to your destination?

CAN YOU STAND THE TEST

As a young boy, I often had to take tests. These tests were a determination as to whether I was fit to move on to the next assignment.

Invariably the test would prove whether I had learned the lesson(s) properly.

There is also another type of test used in manufacturing. In this test a piece of metal or equipment is tested to see if it can withstand the pressure. Can it withstand the weight? Can the object just withstand?

In life we are tested in the same way.

1. Did you learn the lessons taught.

2. Are you adequately prepared for the next level.

3. Can you stand the pressure and weight.

Elevation and success require that you pass all three tests. You have to have all three in place to make the grade. So my question to you today is.

Can You Stand the Test?

CHOOSE TO CHEAT

Several years ago I came across a book called
<u>Choose to Cheat by Andy Stanley.</u> In this book
Andy, goes on to describe that at any given time
you make decisions that put you against your
work or your family.

Andy says that when you put your job first you
are cheating your family and when you put your
family first, you cheat your job. This issue is that
regardless of what you do, You have chosen to
cheat. Some thing is going to be cheated. The
issue is what do you choose.

Cheating requires some hard choices. Changes
in my job. Downsizing my lifestyle. It required
sacrifices. I also had to change the expectation of
my clients.

I had to give away my Blackberry, set-up actual
business hours and not take calls after a certain
time. This perhaps was one of the hardest things
to do. But the benefits have been marvelous.

For the first time in a long time, I can breathe.
I didn't realize that I had been holding my breath
climbing a success ladder. My bonding with my
family grew. I got to share the last high school
years with my boyz pouring into them. And

frankly, being loved on by them.

Life with my wife has improved immensely. Have you ever stopped and taken a look at someone that you have known for years and think I don't know them at all.

We have been able to spend quality time together and really get to know each other at a whole different level. My decision then became very simple.

At the end of the day - did I want financial success and a messed up home life, or did I want a healthy family. I chose Family —

I Chose to Cheat.

DELETING THE EXTRA

Just finished the morning – Deleting 170 Gigs of duplicate, misplaced, and extraneous files. Just like in life, you never know how much extra you pick up in the hard drive of your mind, your heart, and just your space.

Misplaced –

Over the years I have dealt with feelings that, although not detrimental to me, were in the wrong place. Misplaced feelings or emotions will devastate your effectiveness.

Not because they are bad, but because they are misplaced. Many times you get frustrated at your family only to find out later that the frustration was related to your job – and you were taking it out on your family. This is an example of being misplaced.

Duplicate –

As a result of having misplaced files, I would often find myself downloading duplicate files (to save time) but only to find that I had 3 or 4 of everything and can't remember which file is the original (right) one.

Duplicate Emails, duplicate files, duplicate

pictures. This one doesn't have to be deep. What do you have in your space that is duplicated? More importantly, what are you trying to duplicate that someone has already shown you the way or invented?

What have you taken from your past and duplicated in your present? It just might be time to clean out your duplicates.

EXTRANEOUS

I found a program that will go through your hard drive and delete extraneous language files. It seems every program you download or load on your computer comes with files for various languages.

Although this seems like a worthwhile endeavor at the end of the day – you will probably never speak Russian or Chinese. I thought I would only find a couple of files – I actually deleted 10 gigs of extraneous language files from my computer.

What are you downloading from the universe that is doing you no good? Some of us download attitudes and perceptions from our friends. We download biases and prejudices.

These are things that are not helping you to get to the next phase of your life. All of these things are not helping you to get to the next phase in your life.

Take a moment to take inventory of your life, your space, your relationships, and see what you can delete. As it certainly made my computer move faster, I promise it will help you achieve your dreams faster.

I ALMOST QUIT

Can I be transparent with you. This morning I almost gave up and quit planting a church. Now while you may not be planting a church you maybe starting a business. I am sure many of you have been in the same position in life on many occasions.

I mean, donations and finances haven't been going well. Attendance has been minimal. The attacks on my company and family have been excruciating to say the least. So I found myself in a position of absolute desperation and depression.

I really was at my wits end. I thought to myself did I really miss God on this? Why isn't He talking to me? Why aren't the funds coming? How can we have a church, if there is no money and no people? Am I sure God called the right person to lead this movement?

Several times I was tempted to get on the phone and call my pastors and tell them I am finished, I am going to back to running my company full time or even going back into the legal field where I could at least get an advance or something. But I couldn't pick up the phone. I still heard a small voice saying you can make it. (who said God had stopped talking).

This morning After dropping my wife off at her early appointment, I wanted to listen to the new Beyonce album - Her song "Love on Top" – just kept playing in my head.

As I waited for my playlist to update on my iPod – I played a podcast from Perry Noble. WOW did it minister to me. Here are a couple of things God said through Perry.

Strategy over Spirit Sucks

If God has declared it, you don't have to pray about it. Just do it! (going to preach that one day)

If you can accomplish your Vision without God's provision, He may not be in the mix.

Listen to God and Do What He Says

God never calls us to do things that are easy.

If you are following God it is always going to be risky. You are always going to feel like your back is to the wall.

God Never Called You to Play It Safe.

Some of you know – I am a Big Thinker – a Big Dreamer, but a slow doer. My style is to pray about it, plan it, strategize it, then hold it in so long that the urge to do it goes away. (Just being honest). I often suffer from analysis paralysis. Which I now know is a complex to be perfect and a fear of failure.

This church is a major undertaking and I am seeing that some of my old habits are creeping in. I have for the past few months been slowly putting this movement together. Being very careful. Perhaps overly careful. Not because God told me to, but because I was afraid of getting it wrong.

A good friend of mine gave me great advice the other day. He said

"Get out of the way and let God Do What He wants to do. (here is the key point)

You Just Agree."

So I realized, God had been speaking LOUDLY. It wasn't that He wasn't doing enough. I wasn't doing enough. In fact, I was playing it too safe. God doesn't bless fear. I was called to do radical things, which requires doing radical things. Let me take that back. It requires just **Doing**

What He Says.

BIG DREAMS REQUIRE BIG ACTIONS

<u>God is Bigger than any mistake You can Make.</u>

These words have set me free. I am turning in my fear membership, my desire to be perfect, and procrastination card.

We are turning up the fire. If we sink we sink Big. If we succeed we succeed Big. In all of it God will get the Glory. YOU DOWN?

READY – SET – GO

20 RULES

This is not my usual, but I believe it will add some value to the conversation. While surfing the net the other day, I got into a discussion with Tony Steward from Lifechurch.tv. He had a blog post on 20 rules that if used everyday/week would change our lives or strengthen our walk. Tony challenged us to create a list of our own. So here is mine.

1. Spend time in prayer/study/meditation

2. No sodas, just water

3. Limit coffee to 2 times a day (3 on a long day)

4. Exercise every day

5. Make sure I spend time with my wife

6. Make sure I listen while my wife is talking during those times we are together

7. Spend quality time with my kids

8. Clean out my inbox of emails

9. Create a batch time for reading my RSS

feeds

10. Learn something new about God/life

11. Just learn something new

12. Create a to do list and stick to it

13.　Turn off the Internet for at least an hour each day

14. Go outside for a little while – take in the fresh air

15. Eat more fruit

16. No eating after 8

17. Go to bed by11pm

18. Take the TV and laptops out of the bedroom

19. Add value to someones day

20. Find time to be nice to someone

Please take time to write down some of the rules you follow daily.

MASTER WHAT IS YOURS

By James L. Walker, Jr.

I Am So On Fire Today —Just Feel like its A Big Game Today and I'm Ready to Get In The Game And Score A Winning Touchdown, or hit the go-ahead home-run or drop the winning 3 pointer. Going in early to Close A Ton of Deals and GET IT DONE!

But I Need to tell you one requirement. You have to Dominate those things before you. I'm a living witness just Master the things in front of you, on your desk, under your control, assigned to you, and meant for you and God will Do The Rest.

I was never the smartest guy or the savviest guy, nor the strongest guy or the coolest guy nor the cutest guy or the funniest guy, but I worked what I had in my Lane and things started to just fall in place.

Before I knew it my space became a block, then a street, then a neighborhood, then a community, then a city, then a county, then a state, then a Nation was watching me and calling from Fox to BET to CNN and clients from LA to NY to Idaho to Canada to London….and all along

I'm simply just continuing to try and Master that before me with all my weaknesses, struggles, insecurities, ups and downs, good days and bad days and let my Master Do the Rest.

I realize now I couldn't stop it if I wanted to as HE already ordained it as the Author and Finisher with A Master Plan For Us! #Master Yours# (not sure who this is for and sorry for carrying on....

but FIRED up early today and just wanted to share and inspire someone...let me know)!!!

ME DAY

I declare today a ME Day. I am sure you are asking yourself, "what in the world is a ME Day?" Well, let's start here. Most small business owners spend a lot of time taking care of others. I mean you have clients/customers and you have to bring in the money.

You have to service your customer base. They are the most important to your bottom line. Right? Well I call a foul on that. Your success is just that, yours. You cannot fully give your best to your clients unless you have your ducks in a row.

If you are like me — we spend so much time working for our clients that when we look around our own business is a mess. The website is out of date. We haven't adequately balanced our books. Most importantly we have not strategized and looked to our future.

I understand — been there myself. So I came up with something to help me along – and I hope it helps you as well. Here is what I do. I declare a **ME DAY!!!!**

While I try to schedule some Me time during my days — I declare a day usually once a month to do nothing but work on my business. I schedule it on a work day and I make myself the client. If I have to, I sometimes pay myself my hourly rate for the day. Sounds crazy, but I want to eliminate any internal struggles I have with closing for a day to work on myself.

A ME day usually looks like this —

Website cleanup - I go through each website — page by page and make changes or corrections. I check links. I use a free service (http://www.brokenlinkcheck.com/). On a recent look, I found that my youtube url had been changed. On another occasion I found that a contact form didn't work. Potentially losing a ton of business.

Social Networks – I go through all of my social networks – making sure all of the branding is in place. Are they all using the right profile photo.

Is my password folder up to date — I use a plugin called (lastPass.com) to save all of my passwords. On some occasions these password get out of whack -this helps a lot to keep things in order.

Update Contacts and Emails – Over the years I have gotten much better at managing emails (check out http://PeggyDuncan.com, if you are serious about email overload) –

But I have a lot of email accounts – so I have to run triage on them. I also input contacts using different devices and while they are all supposed to sync, many times I will get duplicates and need to cleanup my contacts.

Purchases/Funnel Procedures - I take a walk through my sales funnels, email lists, and e-commerce platforms. The goal is to make sure the process has no clogs in the pipes.

I will sometimes purchase a product from myself. I want to know what my clients are experiencing.

Business and Financial Planning, and Calendaring -- My business' Life blood is **cash flow**. I have to know when revenues are coming in versus expenses going out in order to survive. In many cases that requires precise planning on product launches, staffing, and projects.

I sit with a huge calendar, a cup of coffee, spreadsheets, and a calculator. **Plan Plan Plan.**

Staff/Vendor Meetings – I meet with my staff and my vendors — This is where I ask what can I do to make life easier for them. Where am I in the middle, where am I out of my lane? These meetings have proven invaluable, especially as we have relaunched our brand.

With my vendors, we discuss my calendar and where we can create business synergies, improve communication, and fine tune projects. I specifically do not talk about present projects during this time, because it will more than likely send one of us into "fireman mode", ie. putting out a fire. I only want to look at the future during these conversations.

There you have it — this is My ME Day — and I urge you to try it.

MY ROUTINE

Ever since I worked in the law office, I have had a routine that has worked wonders for me. Routines by their very definition help to get you going in a certain direction, even if you don't really feel the urge to do something.

This system allowed me to run multiple companies and multiple offices all at the same time. Although modified a little from my days as a "power exec".

My routine is very simple.

Sunday Night -
On Sunday nights, I like to go through my email and answer any emails I missed during the week —

I schedule any follow-up
Confirm all meetings for the week
Tag (star) any important emails.
Zero out my inbox – In gmail that means I have archived all messages in the inbox so that my inbox is clean.
I also try to pre start or clear any issues or matters that take less than 2 minutes to fix or complete.
Read through the newsletters/promos/blogs that have piled up throughout the week

Monday

On Monday Morning I grab a quick cup of tea (I have given up coffee for a while – Coffee, I miss you).

I go to my whiteboard and I write all of the major projects that have to be completed for the week.

Mark off the ones that are completed.

Move the uncompleted to the top of the list.

Delegate the assignments.

I listen to a motivating podcast or watch a motivating video. Anything that stimulates my mind and spirit.

I have found that by keeping this routine it really sets up my week and I am more productive. What systems or routines do you use?

NOTHING TO DO BUT WIN

This morning I woke up for the first time in along while, with no other project on mind but my own. I was scared, but yet calm all at the same time. Imagine this late in life, changing business models.

You see, I have been so successful in past ventures, that I have lost my hunger. Now being successful doesn't mean there were no hard times or no failures, just I have played it relatively safe. I realized in order to really push myself to my next level I had to deconstruct and start to think like a start-up.

Let me confess, I am a serial entrepreneur. I like starting businesses. I like helping business get started. I love the point when the light bulb goes off, and you see that a client gets it.

I love the art of the deal, putting it together, working out the pieces, and creating the strategy. Hey face it, I like **WINNING!**

Which brings me back to this morning. While I did not have anything to do, I felt the creative blood coursing through my veins.

That was a WIN! I started to see my vision of a new type of company literally create itself as I typed my thoughts. WIN! I felt God talking to me prophetically. WIN! More importantly, I saw the light. WIN!

The light that my life is not over, my projects are not completed, and my work in the world is not done.

Whether in business, ministry, or at home, I have work to do. I posted on Facebook status a few weeks ago.

Byrd is Back. And guess what? **I have Nothing to Do But WIN! THROW YA HANDS UP!!!!!!!!**

STOP REHEATING THE COFFEE

So, I have one of those fancy Keurig machines that will make you just a cup of coffee while you wait. Well this morning, while waiting the 1 or 2 minutes for the coffee to brew, I decided to go to my desk and send out a couple of emails.

As it inevitably happens, 2 hours later I realize I had not had my cup of coffee. Well realizing this, I went and put my cup of coffee into the microwave and decided to send a couple of emails while I waited the 2 minutes for the coffee to heat in the microwave.

Well 2 hours later I am reheating my coffee yet again.

What am I saying — If you continue to multi-task you will have to keep reheating your coffee.

What would have taken me 2 minutes has now taken me 4+ hours. The coffee is not as good as it would have been had I had it when I first made it.

In your business it might not be coffee, but if you continue multi-tasking instead of concentrating on one project at a time —

you will find that it actually takes longer to

accomplish and more importantly when you get to it – it won't be as good.

Do yourself a favor – stop reheating the coffee.

#preachingtomyself

TIME TO STEP UP

I was at my son's school this morning – I arrived at 6:45 a.m. — between that time and 7:30 am – there were 4 fights and a lock-down — I didn't blame the school nor the parents nor society…

I blamed myself. Why do I blame myself? — I wondered if I as a man and a leader in the community had done enough to instill a better sense of communication and unity in the kids of this community.

There will always be conflicts – there will always be disagreements – there will always be disrespect — It is how you handle the disagreements, the conflicts, the disrespect, that will determine success.

More importantly, this morning showed me what I needed to step up – what good is having influence and favor if I only use it for my children. #preachingtomyself

TIME TO STEP UP PART 2

As I sat with my son's guidance counselor and teachers – I kept hearing the same thing over and over – He is a smart kid – but he is not working up to his potential. He is not getting bad grades but he is not getting great grades, which to me is bad grades.

I sat there fuming, thinking of all kinds of nefarious punishments that would ensue when he got home. I mean how could he not perform at peak levels. He has all of the tools needed to excel. The latest technology, great support, and natural intelligence. What could be the problem, why is my son not working up to his potential. Why is he doing just enough to get by, when he has all of this talent and resources.

Then I realized — I don't work up to my potential -

I stay busy being busy – but not always productive. I am surrounded by the latest technology – but have yet to produce a quarter of what I have the capability to produce. I only make a quarter of what I can make financially. I am only delivering on a quarter of what I have to deliver.

I have technology, an incredible support staff,

and unbelievable natural talents, but only live up to 50% of my potential. I had no room to berate what he learned watching me.

Somewhere along the line – I was told I was different – Somewhere I was taught that just getting by was ok. Somewhere along the line I gave up. I decided to be a number 2- when i had the capacity to be number 1.

Does this sound like you? Are You operating at a standard that is lower than your expectation?

HELP!!!!

In order to combat this here are 5 principles that I believe will help turn this situation around.

Acknowledge.
You first have to acknowledge that you have been coasting along – I know you work from sun up to sun down, but if you are like me – you are great at looking busy for the sake of looking busy —

If the truth be known. You could have finished that project in 30 minutes, not 30 days. That leads me to number 2.

Cut out the BS.
BS is anything that may be hindering you from operating at peak levels. Is it your health – is it

your time management – Is it your love of learning – Is it your ADD/ADHD – Perhaps it is your fear of success. whatever it is, grab a scalpel and CUT IT OUT>>> — this is going to be hard – because it means facing up to a lot of things. I almost erased this whole section because it was pulling the covers off of me.

Be Responsible.
With greatness comes great responsibility– My booking manager said this to me the other day — "It is not fair for you to have all of this ability and you keep it to yourself."

What this means is – if you have the information, knowledge and/or talent – you are required to share it. It is your responsibility to make sure others can get where you are.

STOP! Stop second guessing yourself – stop procrastinating – stop perfecting – stop over-analyzing – stop playing around – stop justifying – stop being distracted – stop multi-tasking – stop beating yourself up – whatever it is just STOP STOP STOP – then see number 2.

WEP This is a 3 point process — **write the plan – execute quickly – perfect later —**

Going forward – I pledge to do better – for me not only is my career at stake – but as you can see the career of my kids and their generation is at stake – All because I Won't Step Up! — I think it is time – what about you?

TRY AGAIN

Earlier today, while working out in the gym I sent my assistant something using iMessage on my iPad. While it toiled and struggled my iPad could not connect properly to the wifi. I had full bars but no connection: (that will have to be another post) And so as a result my messaged read "Not Delivered".

I thought somehow that this would fix itself once I got to a different signal. You know somehow, the message would magically send because now I am connected. Well Lo and Behold, when I got into the office and the iPad connected, it still read "Not Delivered".

Not to be deterred, I clicked the little info button next to my message and up popped this alert. The alert is not what is important. It is the instructions underneath that made all the difference in the world to me - 2 words —

TRY AGAIN.

I want to talk to someone who has tried to send a message or do something in the past that just didn't connect. Maybe there is a project or even a relationship that you wanted to work in the past, but it just didn't seem to work out.

Could it be that at that time you were disconnected from the source of your strength.

I mean the bars said connected but the message just didn't get through. Well my friend that was then and this is now. You may need to Try Again.

I am at a point in my life right now where stuff I have tried to set in motion, seeds I have planted, things that I thought would never happen are starting to come back to me. I mean these were things that flat out, failed.

But I am hearing in my spirit, so strong, the words **TRY AGAIN.** So I leave this as encouragement to you.

Look back at your life, look at old opportunities, then pick yourself off the ground — **TRY AGAIN.**

UNDER CONSTRUCTION

I used to think that if I could get it perfect with no defects or blemishes that I had it made.

That was until I realized that the vitality of a community is gauged by the level of construction going on in the community.

Now I relish that I am now under perpetual construction.

WAKE UP YOU HAVE BEEN INACTIVE TOO LONG

Today, I opened up the browser on my computer, as I do every morning. This happens from time to time - it opened to my HootSuite App, which I had left open. For those of you that use Hootsuite you know they have a super great sense of humor when it comes to warning you about things that happen inside of the app.

Today I was met with a graphic that stated-

You Have Been INACTIVE for More Than an Hour!

This was accompanied by a graphic of an owl that was asleep. What struck me, looking at this graphic, was the actual program of HootSuite was grayed out in the back. I could see the information – I just could not see it clearly as long as the program was inactive.

So I said to myself, I wonder how long in my life have I been grayed out because I am inactive? Not only in my life but what things in my life are grayed out because I'm gone away from them and now are inactive.

What I realized is that life is too short and

the vision I have is too big to let things remain grey. If I am to reach the heights I have planned, I must not let my information continue to be dimmed just because I walked away. I must WAKE UP!!!!

So I ask you, where in your life have you become inactive? What do you have to offer the world that is dim and greyed out? My friend, let today be the day that you -

Wake Up You Have Been Inactive For Too Long!!!!

WHY I WORK SO HARD

Like many of you, I have been saddened by the death of Nelson Mandela. While I looked for ways to speak about what his life and his struggle meant to me, I came across this quote from his grandson, Zwelabo.

"When I am just talking about my grandfather, removing the titles and all the work he's done, there's basically what he's instiled in my life, and that's a hard work ethic as it pertains to education". -

Zwelebo Mandela

Zwelebo Mandela is a student at Johnson C. Smith University, which is actually within walking distance from my house. So, I felt somehow connected to him. It was this young man's words that moved me. In fact it is the reason I work so hard.

"When I'm just talking about my grandfather, removing the titles and all the work that he's done, there's basically what he's instilled in my life, and that's a hard work ethic as it pertains to education," said Zwelabo Mandela.

I don't work hard so that you can give me accolades. I don't work hard so that I can be known by men. I work hard so that when I die, I will have left my children and my children's children an inheritance. Not an inheritance of money – but one of integrity, wisdom, and a good work ethic.

I work hard so that when I die, I will have left my children and my children's children...

If you strip my titles, will my life have meant anything to the ones I love? Will my life have meant anything to anyone else?...

If the answer is yes. Then my living has not been in vain. So I work hard and even harder.

TWO WORDS

Over the last few weeks, my life has been turned upside down by two words. These two words have caused countries to go the war, only these two words have literally kept me up all night. These two words, are driving me crazy. Just two words. Dos words. I even say it to you in Spanish.

These words have countries fighting each other yet they have even been the words that have created the greatest innovation. I've been told in my life that words are like pictures.

And in fact pictures are worth 1000 words. And even in looking at what kind of work do I am wrong that these two words could change my life.

I know you're looking at me and reading this, and saying to yourself I wish which it would get to these two words. But first let me ask you this question, do you believe that words have purpose.

Do you believe that words can change your life? Do you believe that words have the power to heal? And do you believe that words have the power to destroy?

In the English language there are over 1 million words. I mean words are used to describe everything. The beauty of a flower. The color of the sky. I mean words wrap you they describe the world that you live in. My friend, words are important. Words are so important I can hurt so much, that statistic say that words are 17 times more hurtful than sexual abuse.

These words are so strong that they can even choke the very life out of you. Are asking this question what would happen if there were no words. I mean would you be able to tell your significant other that you love them. Would it even matter?

Would you be able to describe the taste of chocolate as it rolls over your tongue? Would it matter? The ability to use words it's so integral to who we are we wouldn't even know what is up is down, we would be able to describe anything and yet I know what you're saying to me.

Richard, what in the world are you talking about. I'm talking about two words.

Sorts of the story. So two weeks ago I was sitting on Facebook and I was reading through the posts. And I saw an article that asked this question. What if?

It started to work in my mind so much because I started to ask myself the question What If? What if I was no longer afraid? What if I could

do anything that my mind said I could. What If?
I mean just think about that. What if You could
climb the highest mountain. Or swim the deepest
sea.

What if you could approach that person you
have been wanting to talk to. What if you could
get the job you wanted. What if you could stop
hurting fro past hurts. What if? What If What if?

Close your eyes having think about your what
if _____? I mean look at it and fill in
the blank line. This scared me because for the
first time in my life I was faced with a future of
no obstacles. A future of unlimited possibilities -
A future of What Ifs?

It meant that I was no linger bound where I
was or where I am am. I now have the ability to
be unfettered. Just by uttering two words What If.

So I ask you this question. What if you could?
What if you have unlimited opportunities. What
would you do? In the beginning we discussed
that words can change your life. They can change
your perspective.

So what if I changed the words What If to I
Can. Imagine the possibilities in that one statement. I have moved from What if to I can. I can
move mountains, I can be rich, I can be success-

ful. I can be a good parent.

I CAN I CAN I CAN.

So I ask you — What would you do if you have a what if moment. And further what can do you when your **WHAT IF becomes I CAN.**

SAFETY IN THE TREES

Several years ago we moved from the frosty winter weather of CT to the balmy summer weather of NC.

It was a one of a kind type of move. just picked up and moved. as all must we went house shopping - after looking at several houses we settled on a home on tje outskirts of Charlotte.

It was a perfect house at the time - leaving several acres in CT; privacy was one of my requests. This house was perfect, although not secluded, it back up to the woods. Which meant no one was going to build behind me.

Well low and behold a couple of years later I heard bulldozers tearing down trees.

What I did not realize is that even though I could not see through the trees the property behind mine abutted a major street.

I never thought about the major street because from our house you could not see the street or hear movement on the street.

For months I endured the construction everyday getting a little more upset. What are they building?

It felt like that would be the biggest house I had ever seen until I realized that what they were constructing was a fire station.

There is an area that I considered forest, rugged, and overgrown they built a fire station.

I remember looking out my window cursing this behemoth building until I heard a still voice say.

This is very much like your life. You have overgrown weeds and vegetation that have obscured your vision. That in fact because of this vegetation you have never been able to see that you are closer to the major road than you thought.

You are closer to getting on the highway than you thought. You are closer to success than you thought. Now that you can see better you can reach the road better.

Here is another point. What was built in the clearing that now allowed me to see the road ahead much clearer, was also a building of protection.

Understand this. My trees have been cleared to provide me safety. My help is not 5 miles away. My help is not 30 minutes away. My help is now a walk through the crowded place that was my trees.

IS YOUR HOT LIGHT ON

On the way to an appointment the other day I came across one of my favorite restaurants, and it made me want to stop. I mean I wasn't hungry, but the very sight of this place made me salivate. I felt hunger pains. I felt the need to stop even though three minutes earlier I didn't even have a thought.

If you are from south you have probably had this same issue. What was it about this Pavlov effect that had me wanting this one spot so much. I am sure if yo have ever been to Krispy Kreme then you know what it means when the Hot Light is on.

Let me explain to those that have not experienced this thing called Krispy Kreme.

Krispy Kreme is a donut shop that serves coffee. Not to confused with that coffee shop that serves donuts. LOL. A Krispy Kreme donut is a wonder of confectionary fried delight. It melts in you mouth and the only way to really fully experience it is hot. Which kind of brings me to the story.

You see Krispy Kreme over the years have devised a huge neon light that lets you know when the dots are the freshest. This huge neon lights lets you know that if you pull over right now - there are donuts coming right off the belt and if you get in line you can partake of this wonderful treat.

That got me to thinking. I mean what was it about that hot light that made me want to stop? And, do I have a Hot Light in my business? Something that when people see it they immediately know it is time to buy. Time to stop.

Do I have a hot light that I can turn on that will signal people to stop what they are doing and do business with me?

It is more than just a light - It is a branding element that tells a story. Here is what the light represents and builds

We are open for Business

We are open and our product is fresh

We are open and our product is fresh and you will want to have this experience.

Think about that. Is there something in your business and life that can become your Hot Light Moment, Your symbol of product or experience contentment?

For me I had to go back to my office and con-
template if I have a Hot Light.

LESSONS FROM MY GRANDFATHER

My grandfather had been in hospice for a few weeks. In fact for many of those weeks we moved our offices to the hospice to take care of him.

On the morning of October 18th he transitioned on to glory. My grandfather, Olin Clark, was an integral part of my life. Many times he was the only man and role model I had growing up.

For the first years of my life I remember spending every Saturday night as his house bouncing on his knee. He taught me how to skin a rabbit, clean fish, and even got me to eat possum (only one time). Boy, did he like to eat!

After my mom, my sister, and I moved away, I remember coming back home and cooking him fried green tomatoes. After many years old age started setting in.

It was about 10 years ago when my grandfather came to live with me my family, that I learned some of my life's most valuable lessons. I will share a few with you.

Work Hard

My grandfather was a World War 2 veteran and due to injuries sustained in the war and through hard living, he had to have one of his kneecaps removed and his leg fused together. This meant he could not bend one of his legs. This impediment made it hard for him to get around without a walker.

But every morning I would hear him clacking along the floor in the house going to the kitchen to wash the dishes. I would often ask why do you need to wash the dishes? or Papa you don't need to work anymore let us handle it. His answer was always the same. In that gravelly voice he would say.

"I didn't come here to sit on my behind. I came here to help you out".

Every month when his Social Security check would come – my grandfather insisted that we take him to the grocery store so he could buy groceries for the house. And no matter how much I argued that we had enough food, he would insist.

"I didn't come here to sit on my behind. I came here to help you out".

And so we would pack up and head to the grocery store and pretend to let him buy groceries.

On many occasions, I would have to take my grandfather to the doctors office or to the VA clinic. On every occasion, he would ask to go by the bank because he didn't want me to use my gas and he not pay for it.

I would say Papa it is cool, I got enough gas and he would answer. "I didn't come here to sit on my behind. I came here to help you out". So I would hand him a dollar and let him pay for our usual double cheeseburger after the appointment.

It instilled in me a work ethic. A man that don't work don't eat. And, no matter where you go in life be prepared to pay your own way and contribute.

Look

It was on these trips that He taught me probably the most important lessons of my life. My grandfather would sit in the front seat of the car and just just watch the scenery and the trees and just SMILE.

When I would ask him what is he smiling at – he would reply – "I am just looking". I have never seen any one so amazed at what he saw. So enthralled at the colors. But it taught me to appreciate the beauty that God has created.

To cherish each day, the smell of the air, the

crispness of the wind. More importantly – just stop and look.

Watermelon Watermelon
My grandfather could sing. A deep bass that would rumble the floor. And no matter where he was he didn't mind pulling up a quick song for you.

Many times while traveling he would listen to the radio and just pat his hand on his thigh. He didn't care if it was rap, rock & roll, R&B, as long as it was music he would vibe.

But if you put on a gospel tune it was a wrap. He would grab the bottom note and harmonize with you. And if he didn't know the words he would sing *"watermelon watermelon"*

Or he would sing in Rhythm; *"I don't know this song, I don't know his song"*, but all the while keeping the harmony.

I learned – Even if you don't know the words – still jump in the song. You see – you don't have to wait in life until you got it together. Sometimes you just have to jump in and 'watermelon watermelon' until you get it.

Keep Singing

A few years ago my grandfather's health really took a turn for the worse. After taking him to the hospital the Dr. indicated that he had double pneumonia and that they really didn't think he could make it through the night.

You see, my grandfather had smoked 2 and 3 packs of cigarettes a day for almost 50 years. The weak lungs and the compromised bronchial tubes just meant he was not going to have enough air to breathe.

So he made it through the night and they put him on oxygen tanks to help his breathing. Well about day three or so, when I went to visit, and miraculous thing.

He took off the oxygen mask and started to sing. I couldn't believe that someone with about 60% lung capacity and could barely talk or breathe, had enough breath to sing.

Fast forward a couple of weeks ago at the hospice, he had a particularly hard night, very restless, lethargic, and in fact again didn't seem as if he was going to be with us in the morning.

On the very next day, I am told he spent the afternoon singing with my mother and my sisters. In fact, singing multiple songs, strong and vibrant. How could this be?

J. Richard Byrd

Lesson- As long as you have a little breath in your body, keep singing.

Smile

If you ever met my grandfather there is one impression you would leave with. He was always smiling. He cracked himself up. There were times when he would just laughed for no reason.

Even in his last days. You could always get him to smile. If the nurse tried to take blood, he would ask her if she had money to pay for it.

One night he pulled off his oxygen mask to stick his tongue out at my wife. Just smiling and his smile made you want to smile. It is hard to be sad when the person you are being sad about is smiling. After he passed, one of the nurses pulled my wife aside and hugged her and told her, No Matter how bad a day I was having, Your grandfather always made me smile and feel better. Life

Lesson – People should always feel better when they leave your presence.

Even in pain, there is a way you can learn to smile.

One of my last nights with my grandfather, we sat and watched a boxing match on television. We ate chocolate and peanut butter cake, cookies, and had strawberry ice cream. #dontjudgeme.

He told me I was fat, he told me we were *"doing it right"* He told me stories about him growing up. He told me he was proud of the family. He told me that he loved me.

He told me how much he enjoyed seeing all of his family working in the church for *"da Lord".* But most of all he made me **SMILE.**Every day I strive to live the lessons I have learned.

Life is short, so Stop and Look
Work Hard –
Keep Singing –
Smile-
And Most of all, 'Watermelon, watermelon' even if you don't know the words – Just jump in the song.

I want you to know, the philosophy of my company and my has been and will continue to be *"We didn't come here to sit on our behind, We are here to help you out".* I pray that on the most part, I leave you smiling.

Fasten your seat belts for the journey. I don't know the words, but I intend to still jump in the song.

WATERMELON WATERMELON.

SOME OF OUR PRODUCTS

Gourmet Coffee
4thaveeast.com

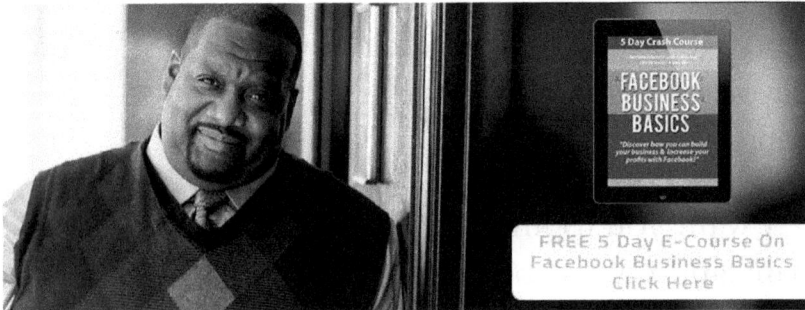

Free Five Day Course of Facebook Business Basics
http://jrichardbyrd.com/fbforbusinessbasics

Top Presentation Apps For Mobile Leaders
jrichardbyrd.com/toppresentationapps

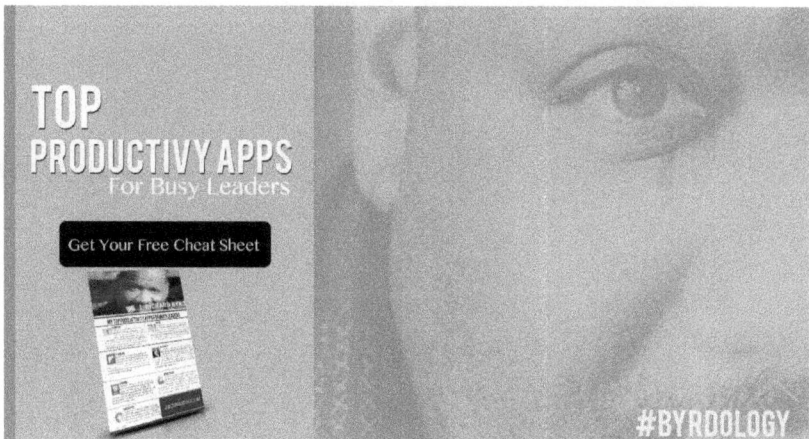

Top Productivity Apps for Busy Leaders
jrichardbyrd.com/productivityapps

ByrdOlogy